The Pied Piper of Hamelin

Retold by Patrice Baldwin
Illustrated by Jenny Thorne

Collins Educational

There once was a town called Hamelin.
It was a big town.

Many people lived in Hamelin.
Many people worked in Hamelin.
Hamelin was a nice place to live in until...

...THE RATS CAME!
Soon there were more rats than people in Hamelin.

The rats were big and strong.
They were fierce and noisy.

The rats did terrible things...

Everybody in Hamelin hated the rats.

So they went to see the Mayor.

The Mayor was worried.
He would have to find a way to get rid of the rats.

The Mayor said that he would pay someone to get rid of the rats.
He would pay them a lot of money.

People tried to frighten the rats away.
People tried to catch the rats...

...but the rats stayed.

A stranger came to Hamelin.
He had bright clothes.
He carried a pipe.

Everyone stared at him.

The stranger went to find the Mayor.

The stranger said...
If I get rid of the rats, will you pay me?

The Mayor said...
Yes, I promise to pay you.

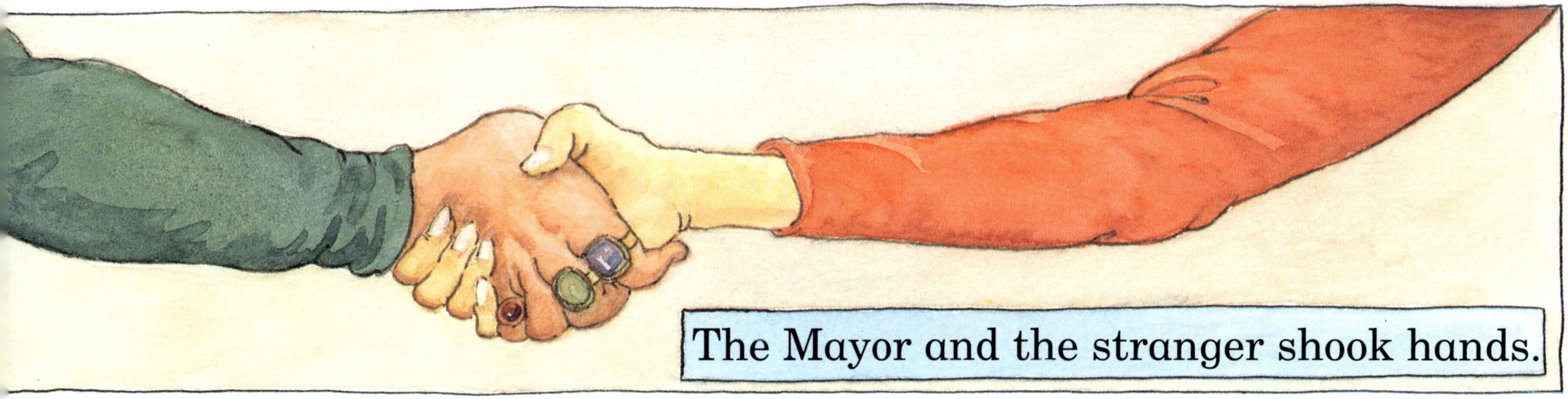
The Mayor and the stranger shook hands.

The stranger played his pipe.
He made strange music.

The rats followed the music.
They followed the stranger.

The rats followed the stranger down to the river.

The rats jumped into the river.
The rats had gone forever.

The stranger went to see the Mayor.

The stranger asked the Mayor to pay him.
The Mayor would not pay the stranger.

The stranger played his pipe again.
The children followed the strange music.

They followed the stranger to a mountain.

They followed the stranger into the mountain.

They were never seen again.
The children of Hamelin had gone forever.